A PENNY FOR YOUR THOUGHTS . . .

Karen Delaney

Life Impact
PUBLISHING

A PENNY FOR YOUR THOUGHTS . . .
ISBN: 978-1-685730-40-6 (Paperback)
ISBN: 978-1-685730-39-0 (Hardback)

Published by Life Impact Publishing
P.O. Box 701403
Tulsa, Oklahoma 74170

. . . here are some of my thoughts,

which were as "stepping-stones"

that marked the pathway for me as

I left the road called "living by default"

and turned on to the highway called

"living by design" . . .

If we would more often share our
“flashlights” with one another,
we would less often need to share
”umbrellas” in times of rain.

Finding friendship is like finding your own sunlight.

Friends bring enrichment
and diversity into our lives.
They also bring challenge,
keeping us from growing stagnant.

May the people and things that influence our lives be wholesome and transforming in nature, not crippling.

Most often, sympathy is devoid of wisdom, and we enable others to stay caught in deadly traps, such as that of self-pity, complaining, the demeaning of others, or one of the real "killers"—that of possessing the attitude of being helplessly victimized by another.

The praise of men has a “down” side to it, in that if we *need* it in order to live, we will be dependent on others for our self-esteem. As a result, our feelings will be owned by others, and we will face instability because we are not leading our lives.

Did your mind ever "hurt"?
Your mind can get overloaded, just as
your stomach can after having eaten too much.
Our minds do not have an endless capacity
for thoughts; choose them well!

The replacing of empty concepts and old ways with new thought processes and responses can become a lifeline to us.

Challenge is a friend,
rather than an enemy
to be evaded.

Have you ever tired of living merely from one event to another? Try living from one perspective to another; from one enriching thought to another.

What takes place *in us*
will far supersede
what happens *to us*.

We are not to betray ourselves in the process of forgiving another.

Forgiveness becomes less of an issue when we are more in charge of our lives, in that we hold ourselves responsible for what we allow to take place in our lives.

No other human being is worth becoming so "big" in your life that they consume all of your time and mental energy.

Humility of spirit without
a balanced respect for your
own identity and uniqueness
as a person can destroy you.

It may feel awkward, at first, to leave a well-established comfort zone for a better quality of life, but you will end up really feeling whole on the inside.

Become congruent
with yourself.

The thought of simplifying our lives may at first scare us, because it seems that if we eliminate the meaningless, there will be nothing left!

Emptiness can be an all pervasive thing.
But emptiness can also be a place
into which real life can be birthed
and authenticity can happen.

I cannot be *led* by my abilities or talents ... rather, I should be led by who I am as a person and where I *feel* I am to be. I may say "no" to an obvious outlet for an ability I may have in order to be where I am to be at that particular time in my life.

Communication should be
for the purpose of relating;
not for the purpose of stating
your "almighty" opinion!

When we do not respect our own feelings,
it seems our only recourse is to
connect with someone else's feelings;
but in the process of doing that,
we lose our own identity.

There are times when your
sensitivity toward others should
not supersede your sensitivity
to your own instincts.
You will know those times.

Work hard at developing and pursuing your personal goals and desires, but not at the expense of another.

A pitying attitude
from others only renders
you more powerless!

Others can do to you only what you allow.

If ever you find yourself exhausted, depleted
of all mental and emotional resources,
you may have given away the core of
your being in the process of
helping and serving others.

If we live in the areas of our strengths,
the more energized we will be;
the more centered we will be;
the more effective we will be.

If you do not define yourself, others will.
But they may define you according
to their desires and needs, rather
than according to your strengths...
And the "humble of heart" usually comply!

Allow your life to be simplified until you are able to relocate who you really are.

As we eliminate the meaningless,
we will automatically be
drawn into our strengths
and into our real desires.

Perhaps the worst type of disability in our lifetime is not that of physical disability, but the disability of not being able to exist outside of our comfort zones.

Wisdom would tell us to look for role models in our lives who can help us “lose our grip” on empty, unproductive ways of thinking.

If we were to begin replacing sympathy
with understanding—the sharing of life-giving
principles—we would all mature much more
quickly, and we could all move through life
with greater flexibility, more resilience
to the negatives which seem to happen.

Seek to be
inwardly directed;
not externally motivated.

When the pressures of everyday life
are combined with insightful wisdom,
character refinement takes place;
maturity happens.

Successful people make mistakes; they fail; they disappoint others. They are just like everyone else except that instead of reacting, *they respond proactively to the negatives in their lives and in the lives of others.*

Life is a process of trial and error;
it is like a tennis game:
a bad serve is no reason for
defeat or discouragement.

The events that happen in our lives
are very transitory; change takes place
often, and many times, suddenly.
But the things that happen to us
on the inside are eternal.

Understanding and wisdom
are as a light to our pathway.
When you find them, share them,
as you would share your flashlight with
a friend to lighten the darkness.

Among your friends,
are there those who
add *dimension* to your life
as well as friendship?

Trusted friends are like
"places of the heart" ... a place
where your heart is always safe.

Have you ever had an attitude of forgiveness toward another only to feel increasingly "invaded" by that person? Perhaps taking charge of your life is the real need.

Being a servant to others
without being in charge
of your own life will
bring you to ruin.

Submitting to another at
the cost of relinquishing your
personal identity and gifts
is a blatant betrayal and
disrespectful toward yourself.

We are to lay down our lives for our brother,
but not our gifts and uniqueness.
The servant in Scripture who hid his talent
was considered slothful and lazy;
he was not commended for being humble
and having the heart of a servant.

No one was created to be a shadow of another or to be the "missing piece" of another person's life.

The realization that we will
end up with the genuine,
can get us through a seemingly
unproductive time in our lives.

It will take time to become choiceful if we have already developed the habit of living by default.

Do you merely do
"whatever is left"?
Or do you creatively move
through life?

Have you become used to accepting whatever comes to you?

Beware of people who make you feel like you are incomplete in some way. They may be coercing you into following their ways—since you are “inadequate”.

I do not know what it would be like to have 101 Dalmatians,
but I do know what it is like to have 101 imaginations;
thoughts scurrying everywhere ... in every corner of
the mind .. .jumping into every window of my soul ...
scrambling into every crevice ... all clamoring for attention.
But, I also lmow what it is like when those 101 imaginations
are gone; it would have to be much the same feeling
as when one were rid of 101 Dalmatians!

You will regret that you ever spent time around people who consider you less than themselves.

If you are not connected to your own self, the only possible connection you may have is with the next moment.

A worthy goal: to become "self-centered", as opposed to becoming other-centered or off-center; not as in becoming selfish.

Most of us need to slow down
so that we can be more observant
of our surroundings; so that we can
better “feel” our way through life.

May my heart be united ... so that what I do, where I go, and the choices I make form a composite picture, sending out a unified, rather than a confused message.

Who is in charge of your life?

Why would I put someone else
in charge of my life,
abdicating the power of
personal choice to another?

Am I a robot, or a created human being endowed with the ability to choose?

I find that if I do not follow my inward instincts, I pay the consequences for it—a feeling of unrest and confusion.

We can learn to choose
a life of awareness and
expression, rather than
one of coping and denial.

I find that when I go contrary
to what my feelings tell me,
I become very tired and
"blurred" in my perspective.

Stay on course—even when you cannot explain to others what is only a feeling!

Why is it that in the process of becoming
authentically who you really are,
you feel you are in rebellion toward others,
and are made to feel that you
are even hurting others?

Life is too short to take a bunch of meaningless detours.

I feel I must allow myself to be unified in purpose, style, and direction.

What would it be like to experience the power of a focused life?

Why would I choose to live a fragmented,
low-energy lifestyle, when I perceive
I could live with all my energies focused,
flowing powerfully in one direction?

A vacuum may not be a bad thing
if it becomes filled with something
new and life-changing. Perhaps without
experiencing an occasional vacuum
in our lives, we would not experience
transition and change.

The most important thing
in my life now is not where I am
or what I am doing ... rather,
am I a growing person?

The only way I can be in charge of my life is to be aware of my feelings, to be able to interpret and act upon them.

If you have completely lost touch with your feelings, you may, *for a time*, need someone to help you make sense out of your feelings at first; but only temporarily. You will gradually begin to be able to sort through things for yourself. You will become used to what your “instincts” feel like.

How does one continue this journey into having a clearer focus and into having more mental clarity if others cause you to feel that the direction you have chosen is “against” them?

As we grow, we will affect the world around us. As we become more authentic, others in our life may feel insecure because we are beginning to respond differently as we become more emotionally healthy.

Growing toward emotional health is not always going to be admired by those around you; in fact, people who can no longer prey on your weaknesses will not even like you anymore.

Try to stay in an atmosphere that is conducive to the growth and development of your internal structure.

Avoid any atmosphere that is suffocating to your inner development.

When we outwardly conform to what is detrimental to us, we cause ourselves great internal confusion and we will suffer loss to our human spirit and to our authenticity.

When you are not in touch with your feelings and not "centered", you tend to always be in a hurry to go nowhere.

Do not let your "gears" become "stripped" too many times by unadhered to feelings ... by going places and making choices opposite to the direction in which you are *really* going.

Did you ever have strong feelings that were clearly insightful and directional—but which you thought you could not follow because others were “in charge”?

Who else is going to respond to your feelings— if you do not?

Can we afford to be paralyzed
and defeated by limiting thoughts
that make us think
we cannot do anything?

We do not always have plenty
of time and energy. We have only time
and energy enough to fulfill
the purpose and design of our lives.

Self-reliance would be an impossibility without self-definition.

Living your life without a well-defined
sense of who you are would be like trying
to navigate life being blind, and always
needing someone to lead your life for you;
sad to say, there are those
who would like to do that.

If we live in the areas
of our weaknesses,
our battery is low
before we even start.

By not allowing our energies
to be diverted, we will be better able
to begin to separate who we are
from who we are not.

When we no longer focus
on our weaknesses, perhaps
we can develop within us the ability
to realize and live in our strengths.

Look for the "something" within that will begin to draw you away from the things you have been doing to merely fill up time—and will draw you to the things and people that fit into your life's purpose and design. This will bring you to the realization of what you are really about, and you will end up where you really belong.

. . . and now, a penny for your thoughts . . .